Opera House Arterial

OPERA HOUSE ARTERIAL

ANNE-ADELE WIGHT

BLAZEVOX[BOOKS]
Buffalo, New York

Opera House Arterial by Anne-Adele Wight

Copyright © 2013

Published by BlazeVOX [books]

All rights reserved. No part of this book may be reproduced without
the publisher's written permission, except for brief quotations in reviews.

Printed in the United States of America

Interior design and typesetting by Geoffrey Gatza

First Edition
ISBN: 978-1-60964-118-4
Library of Congress Control Number: 2012948670

BlazeVOX [books]
76 Inwood Place
Buffalo, NY 14209

Editor@blazevox.org

publisher of weird little books

BlazeVOX [books]

blazevox.org

21 20 19 18 17 16 15 14 13 12 01 02 03 04 05 06 07 08 09 10

BlazeVOX

Acknowledgments

My thanks to CAConrad, JenMarie Macdonald, and Debrah Morkun for reading the manuscript. To Julie Levitt for asking, "What is the opera house?" To Ed Braun for being there and for explaining how a particle accelerator works. And to Geoffrey Gatza for helping the opera house fly, as it loves to do.

coming round what mountain hey
coming round what mountain hey
                              —Anne Waldman

Its crystalline pendentives on the sea
                              —Wallace Stevens

an amusement park ride for elemental particles
                              —Edward Braun

For Ed, who lived three seasons with my "head full of opera house."

Table of Contents

I

Lunatic shift across pediment..15

Opera House Introductory 17
Dark Energy Accelerates the Universe................................18
Catch Me If You Can 19
Opera House Astronomical Critique 20
Dragon as Harbinger of Luck 21
Forest Is a Casino Is Three Trees 22
Opera House Acoustics 23
Recipe for a Solid Opera House 24
Amazonian Interstitial..25
Soil for Peach Trees 26
Opera House under Moon Bridge 27
Tunnel with Blue Lights 28
Opera House in the Ocean Trench 29
Getting Lost on Everest 30
Research Questions I...31
Spice Island Insomnia...32
Murders Dry up and Go Away 33
Marching through Georgia 34
Wounded Soldier in Horse Country 35

II

More fun than a light-emitting diode 37

Her Skirt Becomes a Parade...39
Basement Apartment 40
Blind Date..41
Kaleidoscope 42
She Procrastinates about Naming Spiders 43
Carrot Loves Aurora Borealis 44
Your Kitchen Is the Humboldt Current 45
Gastropub..46
Suburban..47
Threesome 48
Opera House Three-point Landing 49
A Wall at Home..50
A Lack of Consensus without Remedy 51
Opera House Big Top 52
Dusty Liar 53

Stealth Negotiation 54
Research Questions II 55
Cellular Politics 56
Lady 57
New England Skeptical 58

III

Sequence of black chandeliers 59

Noontime 61
Curriculum 62
Prescription Drugs in Farmland 63
A Career in Design 64
Faulty Research among Flatworms 65
Before, Terror Attack, After 66
The Prehistory of Health Care 67
Heavy Drugs for Knee Surgery 68
Motherless Undertow 69
Magnetic North Takeover 70
Research Questions III 71
Lake Erie Wind Farm 72
The Last Color Is Cobalt Blue, Not Black 73
Circle of Words 74
Particle Fun Time Accelerator 75
The World Ended Like a Bad Movie 77
Coda 78

Opera House Arterial

I

LUNATIC SHIFT ACROSS PEDIMENT

Opera House Introductory

Opera house
loads itself like a gun

unlicensed   zero-sum critical

opera house gives you a solar system to inflate and construct in buckets
no-win sky venture

now you see it
                                        if you see it
slicing up the horizon
                        access-denied birthday party typhoon
now you don't

opera house gives you sand where there isn't a beach
reverses sea and sky so each one's creatures inhabit the other

look out below
if you stand under it angels become bladed clothespins

this is what they call Sphinx riddle
subduction
wrong-headed charm
arsenic spindle

fateful twist where somebody waits with scissors.

Dark Energy Accelerates the Universe

Sun maps itself over a street corner
where vision crosses the line of opera house
                        onscreen vector modeling expansion

what physics does to your mind is a flannel shirt
the best jewels in your collection are exploding slowly

light from the opera house moves at its own speed
bending the horns of space
if it runs like a horse you're shaped like a saddle

meteors fuel the construction industry
we're all made of sunset
                Milky Way an iron cogwheel

                        alpha

                        . . .

                        omega

                        . . .

                        sandblast

your cells fly apart filling you with space
can you stretch around the opera house and see yourself?

                        the usual commute
                brightness down leafy street is a supernova

atoms race in their own directions   runaway cattle
opera house keeps moving in and out of existence
                dark matter isn't something we can take home and soak

the best cells in your collection are exploding slowly
what physics does to your mind is a solar wind

                        omega

                        . . .

dark energy drives the opera house into your face

                        ritual particles

Catch Me If You Can

Catch me if you can I'm the opera house
nor mouse nor moose nor hoose
I'm species opera, variety rogue
I'm the opera house, catch me if you can

I'm gingerbread but not
my balcony white sugar my pediment candied fruit
carousel if you look hard enough

                              opera house benediction hazard
catch me if you can

surprise bite into black pebble
ionized context your own dumb luck
release actinide panoply inside your mouth

stone furiously opera house in circles in circles round blackberry bush
                 angular momentum had nothing on this

Opera House Astronomical Critique

When the opera house watched the Big Bang it said, "Nothing will ever come of this."
Was it right?
Discuss and debate as a group exercise.

Dragon as Harbinger of Luck

Opera house is the dragon head at the end of an alley
dragon coming around the corner has an opera house face
opera house at the end of the planet is a headless dragon
all your good luck dragon spoor is a basket of opera house
dragon head coming at you is the opera house disguised as cardboard
red and gold cardboard is the opera house version of a dragon head.

Opera house at the head of the planet is an endless dragon
red and gold dragon is a cardboard version of the opera house
cardboard head coming at you is the opera house disguised as dragon
opera house at the end of an alley wears a dragon head
dragon coming around the opera house has a face of corners
all your good luck opera house is a basket of dragon spoor.

Forest Is a Casino Is Three Trees

Opera house lines up trees in a slot machine
throw us off course   dense pack no light between leaves

                    black on purple
                    yellow on green

                                        opera house knocks out coordinates

low comedy of treetops they look like poodles
forest is a casino or a forest you can't see it for the trees

                    orange on blue
                    pink on scarlet
                    brown on gray

                              opera house comes to life gibbering in a backpack

three trees dense as column inches there's no dense without white space
three strikes land you behind bars forever but what counts is between trunks
                    where the money hides

            opera house gives directions in revival frenzy while we tread circles all night
                    get lost see who notices

it's the money it's all the colors they paint money
falling out of our eyes there's only white space

            all the money colors are hiding between trunks

Opera House Acoustics

NASA chose the opera house to capture planetary music. Its acoustics were renowned for their purity.

     absence of air

Patrons traded their season subscriptions for a program in transorbital freefall. Those with better seats could watch Saturn's rings as they listened.

     frost
         arpeggio

Some heard lemons singing, others the early-morning screech of spinach, others the satisfied hum of flowering cherry.

     chromatic scale

Forty percent of the audience remembered hearing color instead of sound. When asked what color sounded like, they described a variously layered sequence.

     eventual fragmenting

The opera house microphones had been tested repeatedly and declared fail safe. No explanation could be found for the lack of consensus.

       minor key   magnetic   echo

Recipe for a Solid Opera House

Sometimes the opera house wavers
more gel than marble

strain through fine mesh to press out its liquid
opaque iridescence your goal

> a touch of abalone   micro-elastic
> antique hinge buffed with experience
>
> > > unique to paradise

think of kissing through binoculars on a street of flowers and spite fences
how long your eyelashes feel mashed against a lens

> > directional crudity the best you've ever felt

if not solid, re-strain   maintain equipoise
evolution will do the rest.

Amazonian Interstitial

Opera house in steaming rain
brushes the Equator with acoustic white
                        sound waves catching on treetops
                    patience rears like ice under a grate
alights in riverbank red smear
        denial made manifest as a hatchet
                                so much for your rainforest high swing

        promised boat sails upriver leaving you in opera house current
                best-laid plans and all that signage fall down besieged
            research doomed without your autonomic signal
            patience fractures like breakout ice from a calved glacier

opera house interstitial

            Amazon pours through windows onto upper balcony
                all its equatorial horses let loose in song

disjoint forest canopy
venomous cradle

Soil for Peach Trees

       planting peaches in swampland
       where opera house buzzes like horseflies in a holding pattern

                                                       never ripen

Something's going on with the peaches. They start strong but stay green and feel
cold and hard as pebbles.

                                      branches tented with webs

       here trees will flourish
       where tigers walk out of a stream to the summons of jade
       opera house unperturbed vision

The ground is coated with some kind of fungus. Cleaning it up does no good—it
always comes back overnight.

                                         bitter in their bark

       trees will bear harvest under the hum of opera house
                      durian
                  breadfruit
                mangosteen
       only a cat preparing her boat for summer has such confidence

I've tried organic, inorganic, everything in between. I've tried compost and
municipal leaf mold. What next, a tree whisperer?

spreading

                                                  like
                     around

                                          chaos
          mulch

       visit a man who calls himself Sunset East
       he specializes in baskets of smoke
       watch him become the opera house on a background of pink sky

       flushed peony

Opera House under Moon Bridge

People shop online for bags of nails
wear yellow masks at their wedding
any price for skin-to-skin contact with opera house belly

sailing under high-voltage power lines
half seen through rain   displacing City Hall

fire hydrant among spices

can we trap you under a curved bridge?
you howl at us while gearshifting out of range
plunging your claws in silt

somewhere a promise of hematite

herd us like ribbons blowing from a maypole
sheep in upholstery colors
wildlife rove gladly toward a salt lick

simmering corona near the back fence.

Tunnel with Blue Lights

Profoundly sensitive, the opera house is drawn to water. It searches constantly for
the serrated river that runs around earth, unable to distinguish between myth and
geography.

> in its lounge tunnel under the boatyard
> sucking meat off a ribcage

Failing to find the river that runs around earth, the opera house makes do with lesser
waterways. Instinctively it seeks a dark, muddy place to sleep.

> comes and goes irregularly but calls our city its home
> now the tunnel has a name and an arch of blue lights
> will opera house visit more often if it sees ten-watt bulbs hung in welcome?

There are 206 bones in the human body. The opera house prefers the axial skeleton,
i.e., that of the head, neck, and torso.

> arch over a tunnel doesn't change what happened there
> mosquito yellow or drowned green
> city's night side its mouth always full of dirt

Opera House in the Ocean Trench

Diving bell tolls down earth's crust
                              I can't hear you
flip the Himalayas they won't touch us

          down here where it's automatic
          blasting like landfill

diving bell halogen carriage lamps
          lost over centuries
          one thousand atmospheres

                    flat creatures glide into our lights

we're armored against pressure
with a bank of instruments
don't let numbers scare you

          no eyes   narrow as cell phones

no one has ever gone this deep

echo striking   solid
echoing off   closer

echo
))) opera house (((

coral reef thick sandbar thick thing charging straight at us

distortion how distor
          tion how every dis
                    tortion how every
                              everything distor ev
                                        everything dis
                                                  thing distorts

six pillars
five golden doors
rush of stone vultures

Getting Lost on Everest

Chance meeting at 28,000 feet
hypoxic distance thinking I was alone

              follow the opera house into palm trees
              liner notes for Florida, Canary Islands, Persian Gulf
                                                                      context

                        leans toward the north face

shortcut into Tibet over star-covered mountain
                                              sun / black / serration

                                        something about temperature

                                        silhouette / subtropical / dawn

sun reflects trillion opera houses over the snow
twining down slopes together like the end of love
        twin mirrors
        which came first?

get a picture with my phone but fingers aren't working
signals bounce off the sun
phone and gloves blowing it's a scene from South Pacific
                                              warm sea navigational

nobody ever died on an opera house mountain

                  blackening trail onto the Kangshung Face
                  over Tibet with its vortex of palm trees

Is the opera house Dionysian or Apollonian? Is the question worthy of discourse? of debate?

Is the opera house Apollonian or Dionysian? Does it revel in its nakedness? Does it spill wine and leave a muddy trail?

Does the opera house have a conscience? If so, should we consider it external to classical tradition? For extra credit, discuss the nature of conscience.

What is the opera house equivalent of a brain? Do its preferences have a thought component? If not, is it innocent?

Spice Island Insomnia

Opera house reinvents itself as a slab of ginger
sliding under your pillow now your bedroom's finned like a 747
what happens when you take sleep for granted

leaping all night on a raft of questions what were you thinking?
laid open to an intangible minute per square inch

opera house as oracle unleashes dark muzzle among geese
takes you down rusted pathways to the end of light
it's not light it's leftover gold wrapping paper

happy till time ends on a flat island

insomnia perfume tastes mortal but you're not supposed to mention that
opera house is such a slut for fake light.

Murders Dry up and Go Away

Striking out from a reef
we swam to meet the opera house
you thought it was an island
I had a knife in my back

treading water
we watched a right-angled current
sweep it out of sight below the world

if we ignore murders they dry up and go away
what happens to all that water falling off the earth?

Marching through Georgia

Opera house breaches the border
leaving a cloudy blue band

      across red soil

            raw juggernaut mows down constellations walking the street

moons appear in its windows
change of lunatic shift across pediment
legislated by union rules

            drought and dissection against a backdrop of carousel music

when it lands and takes out Georgia
cotton candy
aftertaste they'll always dispute

           against blazing haystacks

Wounded Soldier in Horse Country

Bring into battle a scrap of paper from a fortune cookie
marching orders issued by Joan of Arc

a horse came charging with twenty-four insect eyes and a single horn
opera house passed overhead showing its foundation of swamp and straw

your knee won't bend
when did it turn to metal?

yellow light fills the concrete yard with urine
people collecting something all night

opera house floodlights a pair of silver tanks
you don't know what's in them but nothing grows here

your text messages trip and fall like ballet in a plowed field
only your skin will carry you through till morning

horse lies calm on an altar of snakes
if you bring a handful of sapphires you may be healed.

II

MORE FUN THAN A LIGHT-EMITTING DIODE

Her Skirt Becomes a Parade

Her skirt plays trumpet fanfare

opera house drawing violet across lawns
refinement in the shade of a minor sixth

her skirt again, amber

sun chases itself around the property line
he topples in a field, lungs thick as ham
                              scenting cloves

her skirt becomes a parade of orange umbrellas
leading behind the facade where glitter

                    some hear a fountain

Basement Apartment

Wake up to a fireplace full of crystal
staring you down first thing in the morning

filter colors glowed through your room all night
that party you gave with opera house as guest speaker
thermal trails after it exited the window

        splintering collective

you never caught on to life at the base of a stairway
encryption replaces coupling but that isn't stated

with opera house in the balance pan
city living weighed less than grave robbery
nightclub language picked up as random sharp edge

        what do you mean, next time?

nothing outside but bar codes
hear them scuffle on the sidewalk after lights out

every detail has its brain
something capable of sliding
polish your mood to the sheen of a fresh fish

        opera house crapshoot on your pitched sidewalk

Blind Date

Enchanted enhanced   multipurpose distinction

he performs a dust cloud while two hands rotate the sun
he's all antlers and tires
shows you his name-brand manhood by opera house light
       draw your own fluorescent conclusion

spiritual disunion favors you in the end

you wanted a left-wing forest hero but you got him
you wanted maple soap and a street where they don't dye flowers
a beam takes half your house but you line your lips in black and throw a party

chandelier hangs from clouds all that's left of the opera house
     he's still performing about wishbones and red cones
while you pretend he's Vivaldi or someone sensitive about art

all the good men are escaping to lie under trains.

Kaleidoscope

Don't question color fraction in a seven-degree universe. There's no justification for that piece of glass embedded in your eye.

      paint flecks around the neck of the opera house

Explanation requires a fabric analysis too specific and complex to understand. You fall in love every time you hear classical music. Why do you keep having sex with strangers in the multiplex parking garage and tattooing your shoulder every time?

      nothing tells absence like a string of pearls nobody wears

She Procrastinates about Naming Spiders

He seduces her over a glass of opera house
she promises to name his entire spider colony
once they're married

in the blue and violet glass chapel
something to do with higher chakras
not sure what but they both thought of it at the same time

they marry in a judge's office with a tray of bagels on the console
strawberry cream cheese for luck
she promises again but calls off the spider deal in her heart.

Carrot Loves Aurora Borealis

       opera house rises over the garden

Carrot excited over astronomy
leaps at winter sky crying "Aurora!"
carrot, how long have you been waiting?

       frozen garden
       string connecting carrot to outer planets
       opera house pulsing in black sky

Solar system depends on carrot as fulcrum
carrot depends on opera house as prime mover
opera house as seen by carrot depends in theory on Northern Lights
outer planets depend on methane, gravity, and extreme cold

Angel carrot, this is infinity
false light without end
snagging firmament from your backyard
you know nothing but ecstasy

       blinded by opera house
       in the cold with no socks

One day someone will use you for bait.

Your Kitchen Is the Humboldt Current

Watch the sea rise and turn into ghost ribbons
opera house blacks out lighthouse

tide runs through stone kitchen twice a day
stove rebirths itself as an island floating south

when leaf-bearing friends arrive you must groom them constantly
we need to talk because we're folding at an unspectacular rate

she carries radishes in her blue palms
radishes glance off her eyelids masking as highlights

identity rumbles from the fish tank
opera house dissolves in chlorine

he sits tableside molding protein over fossil wings
takeoff imminent into sandstorm

glamour of specific biology
is there still room in the back tree?

sea tosses an over-shoulder look of derision or peace
cold fire climbing the opera house.

Gastropub

Opera house lands back street in a three-axle town
thinking it's prom night
parks half on the sidewalk to comb its translucent wings
        colors chase each other up its windows
        more fun than a light-emitting diode

across the street she points from an evolving gastropub
he peers through fried oysters at a bus lying on its side

she's been looking for green eyes in corners and not telling him but there's the opera
house
every eye in the room suddenly green and she can ignore pig-shaped blotches on
brick wall
opera house across the street ripples gastropub light into hard cider
she never went to her prom but now she wants silver sandals and there's the opera
house
        more fun than a disco ball and sexier
        chasing visible spectrum up and down its windows

he tells her she's had too much to drink and it's a bus accident

what green eyes did to her then was more than a trick of light
that smell always of turmeric on fire.

Suburban

We bought it for the opera house in its backyard
arched windows   heroic pediment
bright as a trampoline beside the peonies
theater lights reflecting in pools after the yard rains

        unwritten mission to open portal for deer and rabbit lusting after kitchen garden
                    gravity well folds birds down into black vector arrowed on grain

spite fence neighbor asks if our shed came from Home Depot

make me invisible at mortgage signing
when I question they look at me crosswise
        how long has what been there? opera house?
          there's this place in town they show foreign movies
never mind let's get it done

            perfect chord summons animals galloping up from swamp onto greensward
        theater of animal erections in our backyard courtyard kicking hoofs at art history

        opera house takes off one morning in a 90-degree flight of starlings

empty grass rebounding next to peony bed
spite fence neighbor wants to know where the shed went
offers catalogues
        goddamn starlings you getting another shed or what?

black powder where hero's contrail dissolves in sky

Threesome

Opera house gets between them in bed moth green smelling of pepper
as he strokes its wings fine dust forms a line down the center of their bed
                    paradise gearshift
he can't see her on the other side

                              opera house trembling every time he touches such delicate
            response he can't stop stroking as luminous dust gathers into a choke hold

        monogamy goes to sapphire

Opera house gets between them in bed its ram's fleece creaking hide straight off the
tannery
plunging her fingers she encounters barnyard musk from deep in its foundation
                    stable waste paradigm
she can't see him on the other side

                              opera house bucking in the middle of their bed opens her
                legs to monumental architecture crushing weight on her ribs

        the usual morning trail
        charcoal, red mosaic, astral debris

Opera House Three-point Landing

Ungenerous, she expresses passion through placemats
marriage subtlety her domain
complicity lacking

         imaging a blue-green change
         opera house landing pattern

she can't remember if her sofa is ironic or iconic
more annoying than comfortable but the home is satisfied

  strike root spiky bramble make a place where she can lie and taste sweet thorn

         wind lashes red maple
         only tree out there she likes

her husband spends online evenings lacking complicity
she detests all placemats but the home wears satisfaction like an icon

         is hers an up-to-date life?
         a thousand flying saucers crash through branches

opera house three-point landing on her sofa
 who choreographed that?
offering her a ride it must think she's a fool

         she climbs aboard like Scrooge touching spirit sleeve
         sometimes the opera house is right.

A Wall at Home

Children come to school talking about a wall at home
their parents divorce mid-year

mother destines her porch to opera house format
columned arcade rambles over her tongue   backstory
her children's feet stick as they pass each other on the steps
box of damp eggshell
sparrow bones in a cup

amiable custody share swapping kids twice a week

he never knows what to do with his daughter messy as blackberries
humming a song the aquifer used to play
between school and her father she passes a lake shaped like an axe blade
        lime-blue opera house taste won't keep her safe long

                                        knock some sense into her

home from school again with an icepack
                                subtext again but this time it's half her face
when that eye opens it will zigzag interference all her life.

A Lack of Consensus without Remedy

We take turns drawing the opera house on a whiteboard
we're supposed to think it's elemental but to you it looks like a long car and to me it
looks like a flock of owls
          half supermoon half glacial moraine
          top rung of a beachfront ladder
                              under scrutiny

don't negotiate from opera house balcony or strike deals on its front steps
opposing viewpoints chase beacons around the room
don't sign contracts with opera house anywhere in sight

conference table a shaky crescent linking to estuaries
                              examine for floodline
avert emphasis while opera house balances over our heads on a thin chain
dictator pendulum we'll never agree under conditions

          does it look like the neighbor's doghouse or the dogs of war?

Opera House Big Top

There's a line at the end of shrubbery
where opera house overtakes the circus

charms it out of existence every time
            tigers paint themselves across a pottery moon
            genetic stripes in cross-section

                enchantment has an abalone core that doesn't work on grand scale
                    silly for mountain range perfect refresh for a worn-down big top

            opera house colonizes restructure

            we all get a little sick when abalone betrays in plain sight

more insistent than ants on a leash
            fun like a bloody lilac

Dusty Liar

Insist you don't hear the opera house jangling?
you're a dusty liar

insist on time flatlining like a crow's wing?
black onyx contact says you're wrong   you sorry sack
we were all minerals once

when zodiac took the sign of opera house and crowned it
a few were reborn in black stone
                              implicating crystal geometrics

liars left bubbled under shrubbery.

Stealth Negotiation

Opera house transits Venus like a runaway cloak
sideways into converse flight patterning
displaces occupation levels
          delicately
flowers bloom in the tail of a structure

                    something that used to circle but hit the ground wrong

opera house prefers you look the other way during transit
when it passes you can resume usual slippage on your mud pad
your discretion is appreciated while commerce unfolds in secret
          chorus
                         when you pour milk in a mug of phosphorus
               business forces shake hands across orbital trail

magnetic pulse translation to a snarl of intersections
electricity shunted into pluperfect
          opera house exits the scene cloaked in stealth technology
kicking vending machines our only way out of traffic

                    method waits discovery as a rusted war chest.

Research Questions II

When the opera house appears at weddings, people take it as an auspicious sign because of its vague resemblance to a wedding cake. Are they right or wrong? For extra credit, discuss the medieval practice of sympathetic magic.

Does the opera house confer momentum on illicit affairs? Use clandestinely obtained footage to support your answer.

If two people see the opera house simultaneously in different parts of the world, are they in love? If not yet acquainted, are they in love without knowing it?

Discuss the link between gambling and romantic love. If the opera house appears three times in a slot machine, what are the odds that romance will follow?

Cellular Politics

In this year of cellular politics
what happens inside a branch is not up for discussion

take a running jump!   everyone's pregnant
your cat is with kitten and you're with child
comfort gathers around the national table

        trees flowering into dissolution
        we keep making love in a bed of medical waste

voters report to the opera house with state-issued ID
sail blinded into power   faith will reward you in time

insist on hope's gate and risk violent encounter

animals visit us pregnant across species
bless every confinement as a newly arrived god
it may seem cruel but you don't grasp the issues

        inside every branch a crematorium
        no music sounding from the opera house

Lady

Opera house paddles across her dressing table on duck feet
she's awake to possibilities of red and green that make up her face

        it's not her city anymore
she still owns mother-of-pearl glasses
after it rains her dresser reflects theaters from across town

indecision recalibrates as traffic   leveling importance
she can't make up her mind without the opera house
        outside her dialect lungs burst at the turn of a crank

opera house shape-shifts into red disk
she looks through it to the crater she calls heaven
infinity something she keeps in a box of loose powder

sometimes she'd rather die on all cylinders
her mirror conjures smoke from an iron bucket

she sinks her hands in cream
goes out later with the opera house on her shoulder
nothing left of her apartment but one door and seven oceans.

New England Skeptical

Opera house finds New England skeptical
swampy Colonial town doesn't like weird
                              neogastric distasteful

fox cry on riverbank happens every night normal
opera house flirts with neon green

wraparound skirts gather in Massachusetts
quick assemblage near the corner store
colonies won by trickery prevail playing it straight

                                        opera house intrudes on morning sequence

            lime-green squid climb out of the river
                              walking spindly
          tango structure

opera house it's a flirtation
                              tangent
                                                          quirked eyelashes

            tango or is it mango?
                              tangential
                                                          sequins

omnivorous tropic

III

SEQUENCE OF BLACK CHANDELIERS

Noontime

Noontime oppression of plazas

opera house blots out hot dog stand
confuses law clerk looking for lunch on the run

future depicted in a downtown spray
obsessive attention to pink sneakers with yellow laces
                    fountain collision

    Sidewalk search continues for the china egg that went missing last night. Whoever
                    finds it can trade it for a paid holiday.

opera house delicate under skinflint sun

support staff at a plate-glass window full of sandwiches
one in a panic the other hungry
                    collision narrowly averted

 Found holidays and any associated objects are usually reclassified as lead poisoning.

sometimes the opera house is made of bread
if you hollowed it out you could pour in soup

            no room for foolishness eat and run before your job crackles

in bright sunlight the plaza skids to one side
some people blame lunchtime zenith for their troubles

    Moons heave under cobblestones releasing opal mines or minor earthquakes.

man stubs out his cigar against the opera house
he's burned a hole in the sky

Curriculum

They sent her there because it looked most like the opera house
it offered intensive math and a brook ran behind the hockey field
                                              there are no disabilities

    combing through grass for the missing coordinate

any kid can stick wings on a clothespin but it's not a quadratic equation
bend paper clips into a halo but never learn to knit a trapezoid
                                              only deficits of character

    catching snowflakes are they really all different?

when she threw up in the corridor they sat her under a glacier with a bowl in her lap
she summoned the Star of Bethlehem but saw only the opera house

    bird topples off a railing
                                        reversible with proper discipline

architectures flattened around her into cardboard footprints
she always got lost because she couldn't learn to read a map

    that spot near the brook where pesticides

Prescription Drugs in Farmland

You're off again winding something

                                               pimping your bedtime story
handful of sharpened melon

you crated Noah's Ark and moved it to the Midwest
are you inventing a weapon?
your resolve to go off lithium, conceived in a gravel driveway at dawn

       light veers toward you in opera house format
       runway dodging a hat flush with corroded wings
       egret or aluminum

                              you're really there against a scrim of combines

light re-forms as a fatty acid striking the house
where you don't remember spending last night you thought you invented

circadian rhythm broken spring in the driveway
whistle-stop fiction
sound of underdog trains

A Career in Design

Cells roll off the opera house into your living room
culture them into modular furniture with angled assurance of oak leaf

ambition comes to be interviewed

suspension bridges
parabolic shoes

your old armchair resets itself as glass fruit
CD case fills with tobacco
recall your life as a fish before you surfaced in this room

fibrous orientation
archeology of plastic mats

don't be afraid to dream big
redesign national borders with an eye for elegance
create signature pigments to redeem gray soil

adapted for zero-G

harness your charm fish to Neptune's trident
calliope music follows your every design.

Faulty Research among Flatworms

Everything made of red glass

lost our way among chromosomes
genes for grant proposal unexpressed
research dissolves at cell level

we're less complex than a flatworm
                              are great truths simple?
everything made of red glass

experience breakthrough
we scramble informatics in a stick-free pan

let's grab a drink in front of the gold medal wall
where I see the opera house hovering and you pretend you don't
everything made of red glass

come stand under it for luck
toxic in the shadow spores cast

                    heritage map opens boldly into a trumpet

my arteries tangle like snakes
everything made of red glass
whose cell phone stalks me while I map my genes?

we can track them at night by their color-changing pocket lights

everything

did we hack the pattern cells made sifting down a corridor?

of red glass

Before, Terror Attack, After

Survivors recall the opera house hovering over subway tracks before the first bomb went off. Enough were left alive to provide a statistically significant consensus.

      contrary-to-fact explosive

A cell phone may or may not have been used in the attack. The social networks have been cleared of any suspected involvement.

      insect thought based on salt shaker

 A few witnessed the opera house veiled in cinders after an entire block burned. Others reported only smoke and smoldering embers.

      echoing off mortar

Some heard faint fragments of an aria.

The Prehistory of Health Care

Opera house crashes the hospital in a streaming paint shawl
ancient health care prophecy wailing behind it:

        pain shall reveal itself as a color of dissonance

random ether bombs uncoil in stairwells
diphtheria spreads by rumor through supply closets

opera house wraps the hospital fast in its shawl
drops it onto an ashen place or is it icy?
      ribs outlined on architecture

here people are scarcely human
epochs heave underground waiting their turn

backward slide down slate wall
renewed culture of trilobite
      medicine gives way to fossil vet care

opera house redraws time as a painted column
options narrow to a drop of water in a salt box:

        they shall be kept alive to feed on the after.

Heavy Drugs for Knee Surgery

Opera house offers pain meds in place of belief
balance equates with bland cure
seeking streaming video they discovered fire
           oracular serpentine

salmon comes first
I'm me comes first
bully-boy style improv comes first   cracked alabaster
                                                       they're all declining
   opera house comes first in small hours when cats fly over fences and fences fly over
                                       cats

shape of knee pin before meds get to it
shape-shifting metal sheets
opera house cloaked in lilac steel tries out a bold new look

         opera house:
                 my role is distortion pre-surgery or focus on surgery
                 trickster dimension the best narcotic

it's five o'clock but which one? in sky made of urinals
Amtrak station equals anthrax patient
opera house metal breathing

twice around for its open soul

Motherless Undertow

Shutters open and close under the opera house
if we sleep one night in our jeans the sea will run riot

                                        motherless undertow

skyline color of tragedy   synthetic violet

we go home via fossil wiring
our memories the stuff of antique hope chests

                                wet dog shakes rain on the kitchen

opera house barely visible by starlight

                            childhcod linoleum and a zipfish kiss

archived in a long eon of sky

tepid winter sets off streaks of iridescent decay
puzzlebox plants halt at window's viral rim.

Magnetic North Takeover

In far north cabin deep with bear smell
men get together to sketch the end of the world
                              subject to revision

green-black opera house locks onto horizon
cries wendigo intent in an Arctic voice
quick lightning in its windows erases iron

broken compass needle shoots toward the horizon
they've calculated life support after terminal winter
                              based on percentage
cabin wall bending into their backs

                  magnetism under opera house pulldown

      heavy feet cross the roof
      sound like owl wing sound like a covered mirror
      pressure exponent crushes log walls

this time leaving blood traces on shingle isn't enough
when they figured price they forgot the stretch capacity of wood
            year's worth of atmosphere in a single opera house day.

Research Questions III

The opera house has been accused of war crimes by a hypothetical tribunal. Support or rebut these accusations. If you side with the prosecution, how should the opera house be sentenced?

Discuss the role of the opera house in the Children's Crusade. Formulate a theory explaining what became of the children. Could the opera house have saved them? Did it sell them out?

Has the opera house ever been involved in civilian casualties? You may cite archeological evidence to support your answer.

What was the role of the opera house in ending life on earth? Was extinction limited to humans or did it include all species? Answer the question using statistical analysis.

Lake Erie Wind Farm

Opera house landing in a wind farm near Lake Erie
offers music in trade for bladed folklore
                                        what it knows of song
wind passing over cows echoes munificence
touches opera house in a new place

                                                            effect
                                            lake
                            upended
                wind
        turbine

first crush reels opera house in a glacial spiral
undone by knee flow of cows passaging through grass
low on horizon a silver circle oscillates to the turn of blades
opera house balancing in wind as ring chimes not so

opera house:
                why have I never been in love?
opera house:
                silver bears witness to immediate undertaking
opera house:
                if this were chess what would be my next move?

                spinal rattle   orchestra pit
                        from deep in

opera house:
                when I listen to myself I hear empty paint cans
opera house:
                no experimental variation can survive on its own
opera house:
                when the world ends this place will be first or last.

The Last Color Is Cobalt Blue, Not Black

Window plants turn to acid green waterspouts
opera house live ember in doorway
                    presence heady as jello shots
dissolve communicates backward to hydrogen
toxic ultrasound hammering all night

only the opera house could cast a sage blue light over cobalt waste
what to make of this tableau? tragedy or spiral?

how we love it between dice
where things pretend to happen
future conceived as a sequence of black chandeliers
                    obsidian glide
boxes open into boxes open into

                    opera house with tattooed eyes

veering off course we suppose for a reason
crowing like a coach inside a jeweled egg.

Circle of Words

                                    words

                of   will

        circle   not

        a   defend

                house   the

                            opera

[Note: Exclamation points are read as clicks.]

Particle Fun Time Accelerator

For its own amusement the opera house will be discharged through a particle
accelerator. A spectrum of opinions have been voiced regarding the outcome.

homegroup abundance of prickles
        honeycup cactus
                        atmosphere   atmosphere
it's all in fun in fun

                                                        atmosphere
troposphere blogosphere ionosphere

Controversy centers on the planned collision of the opera house with itself. Such
violent extremes of self-knowledge have never been attempted in a particle
accelerator.

                                                opera house barrel roll
                enter Niagara Falls   (puncture)
mirror mirror who's got
        paperweight paperweight universes coming universes
            gnashing steel bulldog steel bedbug

                    subtropical frog barrage

                                        heart trick opera house arterial
mud mud multiverse
        beware sharp things in mud

A cadre of particle physicists have proposed that opera house reflexive collision
could destroy the world. The public is advised against panic. Simulations of the
chain reaction can be accessed online and downloaded.

mud we all are
                        infinity   plus   seven   veils
        dance

                    infinity !! plus !! seven !! veils
                          !   !!   !!!   !!!!   !!!!!
        dance

                                        dissolve

prismatic revisit
    re-re-re-revisit

                    fractured baying at the end of all things

The World Ended Like a Bad Movie

Opera house in water glass near the microwave
                        content with worshipping goats, trees, ill effects
        ignoring the case they're building about the end of the world
        best served by a shared psychosis
water would dissolve it so opera house takes life easy in dry
        litigation possible with the right fumaroles
        trauma changes the law but opera house is in deep taxonomy
kicking back inside a dry clear
                                if any of us were left living
                cinematic universe would score our fingers with thread
        nothing left of us but a light-filled basin
        revenge best served loose on a bed of steam.

Coda

Sentenced to hard labor after the world ended
the opera house flew away
honking like a goose

photo by Edward Braun

Anne-Adele Wight is an active member of the Philadelphia poetry landscape. Her work has been published widely and featured at many local venues. She is the author of *Sidestep Catapult* (BlazeVOX, 2011). The opera house has followed her around since 1983 and only recently agreed to show its faces.

Made in the USA
Monee, IL
07 July 2026